TABLE OF CONTENTS

300 BEST JOKES – FOR ADULTS ONLY – BOOK 2

My grandpa is 89 years old. One day we went to the mall with him. Suddenly I noticed he is staring at a teenage girl with an acid yellow mohawk. The girl noticed his unwavering gaze and asked him, "What's up creaker? Haven't you ever done anything crazy?"

My dad replied: "Once upon a time, I was drunk and stoned and I had sex with a parrot. I was just wondering what if you are my daughter."

Don't forget to capitalize people's names.

"I always help my uncle Jack off a horse…" and "I always help my uncle jack off a horse..." makes a huge difference.

Every couple on real estate show should say that:

"I am a part-time Chinese food delivery man, and my wife grows lettuce in the garage for a living. We are looking for an exclusive lower Manhattan penthouse loft, and we have a budget of 17 million dollars."

- My best friend was single until the age of 45, but then he suddenly got married.

- What happened?

- He went to the ski resort and broke both of his arms. When he was recovering, someone had to open his beer. That's when he met a young nurse who was good at opening beer. Eventually, he figured out she is also good in something else he could not do alone any longer with both of his arms broken.

- That's the sweetest story I've ever heard!

"I'm in a naughty mood… Let's take this girl to our bedroom as well…"

That's what I whispered to the bottle of wine.

Sex is not the answer. Sex is the question. "Yes," is the answer.

4

Instant messaging with a friend in 2040:

- Did you hear that 20 years ago there was life outside the Internet?

- Bulls**t. I need proof!

- How do I get rid of split ends?

- Ok, listen attentively. Take a tablespoon of wild honey, add a pinch of baking soda and a teaspoon of coconut oil. Stir well and add two tablespoons of sour cream and one egg yolk. Stir well again. Finally, throw it in the garbage and go to the hairdresser.

- Do you think I want to kill you? It is the last thing I want to do.

- So it's still on the list!

- How do I avoid having sex with the wrong person?

- Just do it solo.

- My ex-boyfriend wants me back. How do you call this situation in one word?

- Fiction. You don't have an ex-boyfriend.

I had to tons of hamburgers, pizza, and other junk food during the holidays to gain 20 lbs for a role in a new blockbuster. Then I realized I'm not even an actress.

- What do a vegan at the steakhouse, a pizza boy, and a gynecologist have in common?

- They can smell it, but they can't eat it!

One guy was stoned, and he called to police yelling that someone wants to kill him. He immediately called Domino's to order a pizza. Guess what? Pizza delivery boy came first!

Someday I am going to afford a new Tesla, iPhone with diamonds, and a $5,000 purse like this lady using food stamps in front of me.

- A policeman stopped me for speeding on my way to the office. You won't believe this: he had a steering wheel in his pants!

- What? Did you ask him what's this for?

- Yes, I was like, "Excuse me, Sir, can you explain me, why do you have a steering wheel in your pants?" He replied, "I have no idea, but it's driving me nuts!"

- What's the funniest joke you've heard on April 1?

- I was watching porn in my room, and there was a pop-up message from the porn site: "Thank you! Video successfully shared on facebook, twitter, and LinkedIn!"

I refreshed facebook, twitter, and LinkedIn for several times before realizing it was the April Fools' Day!

I was watching porn and opened another window with javascript tutorial so I could switch between the windows quickly in case my parents walk into the room. Suddenly the door opened, I switched to another window and fell off the chair trying to pull up my boxers quickly. The dad looked at me. I said:

- Dad, this is not what it looks like.

Dad replied:

- Good! Because it looks like you have been masturbating to a javascript tutorial.

- How to figure out whether your girlfriend is cheating on you or not?

- Wait until she falls asleep. Monitor her heart rate while whispering random male names into her ear.

- I love my boss!

- What? I thought you are married!

- Yes, but I work for myself.

My wife never can find her hair ties.

But it doesn't matter because she can remember my exact words in some random dialogue 12 years ago and she knows for sure it was a sunny day, 1:35 pm and she was wearing blue shorts, a white t-shirt with stripes and she was angry at me because I didn't throw away the garbage.

The woman had two female parrots who knew how to say only one thing: "Hey, we are sluts. Let's have some fun!"

They kept yelling it all the time until the woman got mad and brought them to a priest.

- Father, please, advise what to do with my parrots. These ladies talk about dirty things all the time.

- I know what to do. I have got two male parrots that are taught to praise Jesus Christ and read the prayer. We will put your female parrots into their cage, and my male parrots will teach them good manners.

In two minutes, they let the female parrots into the cage with the male parrots that were reading the prayer. Immediately the female parrots yelled out the only thing they knew: "Hey, we are sluts. Let's have some fun!"

One of the male parrots looked at his fellow and said:

- St. Captain Flint, put your prayer aside. God answered our prayers!

- What's your favorite thing in the office work?

- The best part of it is saying, "Bye, guys. I'll see you after my vacation."

The stranger approaches a pretty girl and asks her: "Give me your number, or I will follow you."

- In 1999: the girl gives him the wrong number to get rid of him.

- In 2019: the girl lets him follow her. On Instagram.

Nudes for men are the same things as flowers for women.

The alcoholic came to yoga school.

- Hi, I am an alcoholic. I've read in the magazine that yoga helps alcoholics to change their lives. Can you give me a chance?

- Of course, welcome to the family!

(Two months later).

- So how are you? Have your drinking habits changed?

- Yes, it's a game-changer! All my friends are impressed. Now I can drink shots standing on my head on the bar counter!

Some guy was sitting ten steps away from me in the dark corner of the train station. He was speaking on the phone quietly. Suddenly he yelled loudly, "Listen, Alicia! I will tell you a secret. Only me and Janice knows. Me, Janice, and now you…"

At this moment I realized he's talking about me! I am Janice, and this guy is Ryan, my friend. I had no idea who the heck is Alicia and what is the secret about, but I stood up and yelled, "Wait a minute, I did not give you my permission to talk to her about the secret!"

The appalled guy looked at me. I made one step closer. It wasn't my friend Ryan.

Getting friendzoned is like running a 99-yard kick return to find out there was a flag on the play.

Boy:

- Hello.

Girl:

- I know you are lying!

All I want for Christmas is you(r cash, credit cards, car, house, time, and life).

- My friend Sasha is 32. She is beautiful and smart. Not married. She doesn't have a boyfriend, but she never sleeps alone.

- Why?

- Sleeping alone is such a waste of her sexual talent!

I go to the gym. One guy often arrives at the same time as me, and we spend a few minutes in the locker room. I don't even know his name. The other men often speak about girls, bodybuilding supplements, and random things about their life. On the opposite, this guy always speaks about the weather. Yes, I know, there are lots of people who may say something occasional like 'what a nice sunny day' or 'this rain ruined my weekend plans' but this is not the case. This guy is silent all the time. When he opens his mouth, you can immediately guess he is going to say something about the weather. Finally, I got pissed off and told him: "Dude, you always tell us it's warmer today than it was last week or some crap like this. But what's the point? We all know what the weather was last week. Tell us something else. Tell us about your job, for example! What's your occupation?" The guy replied, "I am a meteorologist."

Geography lesson at high school:

- My mom purchased a very nice scarf. Mr. Hayden, can you help me to find on the map the city where this scarf came from?

- Sure, I know all the cities in the world. Shoot.

- So where is Woven located?

- Woven? Are you sure it's W-O-V-E-N? There is no such city in the world!

- I'm sorry, Mr. Hayden, but you are wrong. The tag on the scarf clearly says: "WOVEN IN SCOTLAND."

When my wife was 18, and I hugged her for the first time, she felt so soft.

Now she is 38. She is wearing waist trainer and hugging her feels like hugging a robot or a police officer.

- There was a guy at my school who wore black lipstick and was all gothy. Until one day I caught him buying an assvibrator.

- Wait, you "caught" him? It sounds like you were behind him in line at the assvibrator store.

- Oops…

The mobile company has been researching the most anticipated phone options. It turns out many people want to have the feature "UNSEND TEXT MESSAGE." Some of the interviewees claimed they would have paid several hundred bucks to unsend some of their messages.

- This New Year I've had the best New Year kiss ever.

- What? You did not even have a boyfriend!

- It was a kiss with a bottle of champagne. Unlike in all the previous cases, the consequences only lasted that one night.

- If you need a fake boyfriend, call me. I can pretend to be your boyfriend on Thanksgiving.

- What do you want in exchange?

- Nothing. Just feed me.

- Do you know any smart quotes?

- "Send him nudes."

- Who said this?

- Three Margaritas and Bloody Mary.

- Anyone speaks python here?

- SH-SH-SH-SH…

- Ssss-Sh-Ssssssssh…

- Shut up! I mean python programming language, you stupid idiots!

- Call me on Friday.

- I don't have your number.

- Did you lose my number?

- Yep. I lost your number the moment I hit the DELETE button.

- My ex-girlfriend is so mean. She broke up with me last week and an hour ago she sent me this photo where she is with her new boyfriend in the bed.

- That's mean. Did you reply?

- No. I transferred the photo to her father.

- Why did you break up with your girlfriend?

- Her life goals did not match mine.

- What's wrong with her life goals?

- Her life goals are to get 2,500 likes on her selfies; text with at least five other guys a day and drink seven glasses of wine three times a week.

- Luis, you only think about sex! Same one thing every day!

- It's not true! I also think about food and beer every day!

- When my mother-in-law came to visit us, all of us, including four kids, have been arguing for several hours non-stop. No one listened to anyone. It was a nuthouse!

- There was someone who's heard every single word.

- Who?

- Me! I am your neighbor!

Donald Trump and two senators walk in a famous entertainment center. The staff is amazed, and the host says:

- It's a big honor! What would you like to do? We have a casino, a theater, two rooftop restaurants with four swimming pools, Thai massage, spa, karaoke, indoor golf, bowling, virtual reality room...

Donald Trump replies:

- No, wait. We are just going to plan World War III here.

The host is puzzled:

- Really? And what's going to happen next?

- We are going to kill 70 million Mexicans, 100 million Muslims, and one supermodel with huge tits for a start.

- Why would you like to kill a supermodel with huge tits?

Trump turns to senators:

- See, I told you people won't even care if we kill Mexicans and Muslims.

- If we get electricity from electrics, banknotes from bankers, and jewelry from jewelers, do we get plums from plumbers?

- No, but I know many people get morality from morons.

- How do you take s**t to a higher level?

- Poop in an elevator on the ground floor. Press any button.

- Hey, Liz. How are you? You haven't texted me in a while. Are you okay?

- Oh, thanks, I'm fine. Just haven't been drunk in a while.

"I DON'T NEED ANOTHER DRINK!" – said drunk me never.

- Hello, 911. I have an emergency. My girlfriend is about to kill me.

- Is she there with you right now?

- No, she is probably on her way to my house.

- Did she threaten you?

- No.

- How do you know she wants to kill you?

- I accidentally liked some hot chick's photo on Instagram!

- Say no more. I'm sending officers to your house!

The girls at college talked about makeup, but I had a feeling they talked about weapons. For example:

- What eyeshadow did you get this time?

- Oh, this one is Mac 34pro ultra 22 points.

Seriously, the same girl can't remember the name of the U.S. capital, but she knows all these "34pro ultra 22 points" stuff!

- What do you say when it's snowing late in April?

- Fine weather for the 82nd of February!

The teacher:

- Julian, why are you always late?

- Sorry, Miss. It's all because of the stupid sign.

- What sign?

- When I walk, I see it every day. It says, "SLOW DOWN - SCHOOL AHEAD."

There is a hot girl in our office. I sort of stalked her because I was thinking about her 24/7. Yesterday she asked me whether I can give her a ride home. I was amazed, and we had a nice conversation during the ride. Then I dropped her off right in front of her house. She said:

- Thank you! But… Wait a minute… How do you know where I live?

I asked my girlfriend to describe our relationship in five words. She replied immediately:

- WHO THE F**K ARE YOU?

When my baby son drinks from a bottle, falls asleep with this bottle and my wife has to carry him, people say this is cute.

When the same thing happens to me, people ask my wife:

- Why do you carry this stinky alcoholic?

- All right, I busted you! What are you doing on Tinder? Are you cheating on me?

- Of course, no! I am just there to meet friends!

- Oh, really! It's like saying that you watch porn because you want to find out how to fix the freaking sink!

In the camp, my cousin asked to borrow anyone's USB cable to charge his e-cigarette. I couldn't because I was charging my e-book. My brother couldn't because he was charging his light-up glowing shoes. The future is here!

This girl is trying to rush me into a serious relationship. I don't know what she is thinking about. I barely know her, but she is acting like we haven't just met in summer... of 2009.

- How do you understand what is private and what is secret?

- It's easy. When I sleep with my wife – it's private. When I sleep with your wife – it's secret.

English teacher:

- Herbert, tell us where you were born?

- Llanfairpwllgwyngyll in Wales.

A gift for you

Enjoy your gift! Ha ha ha happy Father's Day! From Jason Lukenbill

- Can you spell it, please?

- Wales?

- No, Llanfairpwllgwyngyll.

- Ummm, maybe I was wrong. I was born in York.

- Son, what did you learn in your chemistry lesson yesterday?

- I should not lick the spoons.

- I called you a few times yesterday. Why didn't you pick up the phone?

- Sorry… I don't use the phone for this.

- I got fired from my job at the tea company.

- Why?

- They found out I am drinking coffee during our tea breaks.

A**hole tip: if you have an enemy and his wife gets pregnant, you can use a fake account and leave a comment under her pregnant picture: "Does he know it isn't his?"

- What's the difference between mom and dad?

- Mom always knows everything about her kids: best friends, secrets, favorite colors, cartoon characters, and doctor appointments. Dad is vaguely aware of some short people living in his house.

What if porn ads were not fake?

What if all these years I have been missing out on local single moms that wanted to f**k in my area?

I am filling out the job application form:

- Have you ever been arrested?

- No.

- Why?

- I've never been caught.

- What is your favorite birthday cake topping?

- One hundred dollar bills!

- That's a crazy day.

- Why?

- I have just burned 3,500 calories.

- It's only 1 pm. You didn't even leave the kitchen since the morning. And I didn't see a treadmill there. How did you do that?

- I left cookies in the oven and started playing Minecraft.

The alien came to Earth and asked a wise man:

- What is life like in the world of humans?

- Do you see this cute little kitten? Life among humans is like this awesome kitten. But one day it may s**t in your shoes.

All people need to believe in something.

Speaking about myself, I believe I should live in the Maldives with an unlimited supply of food and cocktails.

- Sometimes I look at my Facebook posts from two years ago, and I want to delete them. It feels like I'm not the same person which I used to be two years ago.

- Oh, my situation is even worse. Sometimes I look at my posts from five minutes ago, and I feel the same way.

- How many IT experts does it take to change a lightbulb?

- Ummm… I have no idea. But I would buy tickets to see this show.

At 4 a.m. I was on a backseat in a taxi on my way home. I played with my phone for about 20 minutes without paying attention to the road. When I raised my eyes, I realized we were in a bad part of the city, and it was in the opposite direction of my home. Then we turned to some odd place and headed to some suspicious garage in the middle of nowhere. I took out my nail file – the only sharp object I could potentially use as a weapon. Then the taxi driver stopped the car, stretched, looked in the mirror and screamed: "Arrrr, who the hell are you?"

This guy forgot that he took a passenger!

- What's your favorite game? Mine is called "Monopoly".

- Mine is called "When is the dinner?"

A cannibal is on a cruise ship. He comes to the restaurant, and the waiter gives him the menu. The cannibal says:

- Please, take away this menu and bring me the list of passengers.

I love living next to the park. I often wake up, look outside, and see all these beautiful trees, hear the birds singing and see people exercising and jogging. It's very inspiring. Usually, it inspires me to get up and close the freaking blinds!

At the museum:

- Maam, it's a disaster! Your son broke a 3,000-year-old vase from Babylon!

- Thank God! I thought it was a brand new vase!

Traci loved Lawrence. Lawrence said, "Traci, I don't love you anymore. Let's be friends."

Traci started posting depressive love crap on her Facebook page.

Traci posted hell A LOT OF depressive love crap on her Facebook page.

I don't know Lawrence, but when I am reading Traci's posts, I start missing Lawrence too.

The family couple noticed a man with a cat on the street. The man held a sign: "TALKING CAT ON SALE – ONLY $1." They came closer, and the cat started speaking:

- Please, buy me. I am a great cat. I know how to use the toilet. I can even make your bed every morning. Also, I'm a wonderful cook. I can even make a cake for your birthday!

The man and the woman looked at each other in shock. They asked the seller:

- Why on Earth would anyone sell such an incredible talking cat for $1?

- Yesterday, I had a birthday, and he made a cake for me. My guests started eating the birthday cake, but then we found out there was a dead mouse inside! He is lying that he is a great cook. AND I HATE LIARS!

- What's your favorite short drinking toast?

- I am surrounded by alcoholics and sex addicts. So happy I have found all of you!

When we celebrate Thanksgiving, Christmas, and my birthday, I have to set a reminder for myself: "Don't forget to set the scales back 10 lbs tonight."

When I start studying Spanish, I fall asleep in a minute.

When I need to fall asleep quickly, my brain starts playing my worst memories from the past 20 years!

A young lady is buying a box of tampons in the store. There is no UPC at the box, so the cashier asks her male co-worker:

- Can you please check the price of tampax?

- Do you mean the kind you push in or the kind you hammer in?

- What the…?

- You said to check the price of thumb tacks. I am asking whether you mean the kind of thumb tacks you push in or the kind you hammer in?

You should have seen the face of the young lady who wanted to buy these tampons.

- What's the hottest thing that has happened in your bedroom over the last few months?

- My laptop burned my thighs.

When you are feeling you don't have enough patience, imagine there are too many witnesses.

When my doctor recommended me to consume more fruit, I decided to drink an extra wine bottle every day. I bet he will be proud of me!

Gynecologist asks the woman:

- So, how often do you have sex with your husband?

- My husband and I have so-called Olympic-sex.

- Oh, it sounds like a lot of fun. Can you tell me the details?

- It happens only once in four years.

When she was a little girl, she learned there are four seasons a year.

When she became a woman, she learned there are only two seasons: freaking cold season and leg shaving season.

- Ozzy, what is "analogy"?

- Probably, a study about buttholes.

Top-3 reasons for dating single moms:

1. Single moms always have tasty snacks in their kitchens.

2. Single moms often have PlayStation.

3. Single moms are too busy with their kids so they don't have time to play the game of nerves with their boyfriends.

An 8-year-old Charley's parents divorced. A few days later he passed by his mom's bedroom and saw her rubbing her body and moaning, "I need a man! I need a man!"

Over the next few weeks, he saw her doing this several times.

One day, he came home from school early and heard his mom moaning louder than usual. When he peeped into her bedroom, he saw a man on top of her.

Little Charley ran into his room, took off his clothes, jumped on his bed, and started moaning, "I need a skateboard! I need a skateboard!"

- Jane, I want you!

- Do you mean you want to become my boyfriend?

- It's hard to say. Can I get a one-week trial?

Little Norah came home from school with a smile on her face, and told her mom:

- Cristian Reeves showed me his weenie today after PT class.

- What did it look like?

- It reminded me of a peanut.

Relaxing with a hidden smile, Norah's mother asked:

- Really small, was it?

- No, salty.

- I have got the tin full of bees. How to determine the gender of each bee?

- Open the beer. Put the beer bottle near the mirror and let them go. Those bees who will go to the mirror are females. Those who will go to the beer bottle are males.

A lady goes to the doctor to complain that her husband lost his sexual desire. The doctor gives her an experimental pill and tells her to slip it into his meal during the dinner.

Next day, the lady is back:

- Doc, your experimental pill worked great! I put it in my husband's soup during dinner. In three minutes he jumped up, raked all the dishes onto the floor, grabbed me, ripped all my clothes off, and ravaged me on the table!

- I'm sorry, I didn't know the pill was that strong! The foundation can pay for the damages.

- Don't worry, Doc. We are never going back to that restaurant anyway.

I found this letter to Tooth Fairy from my daughter under her pillow:

"Dear Tooth Fairy. Please, don't bring me candies. I'm afraid I'll lose all of my teeth if I eat more candies. Bring me money instead. If you have no cash, it's ok. My dad has PayPal. I love you! Rose."

Me: "It's time to go on vacation and travel like crazy in France, Italy, and Spain!"

My bank account: "You can travel like crazy to the places like Burger King, Wendy's, and Taco Bell across the street!"

- How to surprise my girlfriend on Valentine's Day?

- How about this kind of surprise: introduce her to your wife!

Everything I want now is either illegal, too expensive, or doesn't give me her number.

- Nick, what is your mother tongue?

- English, Sir.

- Do you know why is it called a 'mother tongue'?

- Because of my mother's tongue, my father rarely gets a chance to speak.

- Is this mushroom edible?

- Every mushroom is edible. But some of the mushrooms are only one-time edible.

My Chinese cookie advised me today: "Try to live a more adventurous life."

I am trying. It's a pity the cookie didn't explain how to do it with $19 on the bank account.

I'm wondering whether my girlfriend even believes herself when she's saying:

"Honey, I'll be ready in a minute!"

The man is buying condoms, and the cashier is asking:

- Do you want a bag?

- She is not that ugly!

- How to get an orgasm during the party?

- In your case, there is only one solution. Turn on loud music, hold confetti in one hand and masturbate with another hand.

- Fabio, you never go to church. Why do you hate God?

- I hate God? I love God! I hate his fan clubs!

Theodor loves women, and women love him as well. Theodor has a new woman in his bedroom every day. Also, he has a red Ferrari. But today I saw Theodor on a bus.

- Theodor, why are you on the bus, if you have a Ferrari?

- This bus can pick up twenty times more chicks than Ferrari.

A blonde flies on the airplane for the first time. She asks a flight attendant:

- Miss, how high is the airplane?

- 32 thousand feet.

- Cool! And how long is the airplane?

If you need medical advice, ask anyone but Google. It's easy to start from dandruff and get clinical death in just a few clicks.

- Do you say a prayer before eating dinner?

- I don't need to do this. My wife is a wonderful cook!

Cinderella teaches a lesson to millions of girls in the world:

"If you want a prince, come to his house and leave your crap there. If he is a true prince, he will find you, return your crap, and offer his hand."

- Baby, when will I see you again?

- In half an hour, I'll post my selfie on Instagram.

The funny thing about my brain: I remember lyrics to every 90's and early 2000's song. At the same time, I don't remember where I put my keys, headphones, and sunglasses.

And, by the way, why the hell I have just walked into the damn kitchen!

During the job interview:

- What is your favorite hobby?

- When I come home, I put on my pajamas and act like a kid.

- Considering the fact you are wearing pajamas with dicks and the purple unicorn wig right now, it looks like you are doing it outside of the home as well.

- I'm a ninja.

- No, you are not!

- Ok, did you just see me do that?

- Do what?

- Exactly. That's why I'm a ninja.

- Do you like 50 shades of gray?

- I hate it.

- Why?

- The only 50 shades of gray in my life are 50 shades of gray bags under my eyes.

I applied for the general manager position in a large electric company. HR manager didn't even look at my resume, but he told me they are looking for someone older.

That's why I applied again in a week after my 22nd birthday. I did not get accepted, but at least it made the manager look at my resume.

- Don't you hate when you s**t on the floor and can hear it fall but cannot find it? Then you spend minutes trying to find it, and you are also in a hurry.

- WHAT?

- Oh... I mean, don't you hate when you DROP s**t on the floor...

Once I asked my 90-year-old great grandfather:

- Grandfather, what should I do if one day I have a problem that I cannot solve, the next day the new problem arises, and at the end of the week, I have five or six problems that become a pain in the neck?

He replied:

- Remember, grandson, there are no such five or six problems that five or six glasses of wine can't solve.

- How are you? You look excited.

- I have just ended a ten-year relationship.

- Wow, really? Are you feeling okay?

- Well, yes. It was not my relationship.

Wife is asking her husband in the bed after sex:

- Honey, did you have any girlfriends before meeting me?

Husband is not answering. Wife is asking:

- What is this silence supposed to mean?

- Don't interrupt while I'm counting.

If you want to be a perfect wife or husband, you need to learn how to be fluent in silence when your partner gets pissed off.

Sometimes I want my co-workers and boss to learn this skill too!

- Our company has 1,500 employees. How many people do you think work in our company?

- Didn't you just say we have 1,500 employees?

- Yes. But then I asked you how many people work in our company. Not more than fifteen.

The young man at the drugstore:

- Give me 300 condoms, please.

Two girls standing behind him start giggling. He turns around, looks at them, and says:

- No, I mean give me 302 condoms, please.

English lesson for adults in Spain. The teacher asks the students to introduce themselves in just a few words.

- Hi, I am Roberto. I like science. I am a scientist.

- Hi, I am Ricardo. I race a sports car. I am a racist.

- How do you like my new photo with an alien filter in SnapChat?

- Oh, this was a filter? You don't even need an alien filter, dude!

Even if there are screenshots, there are still two sides to every story.

- What's the best thing about being ugly?

- Your phone battery lasts longer.

- Hey, do you sell wallets?

- Yes, look here. We have many wallets! What kind of wallet do you want?

- I need a wallet with free refills.

Teacher:

- Prove this with an example: if A=B, and B=C, then A=C

- That's easy. Your son slept with me. I slept with the football coach. Your son slept with the football coach.

- How to make people think that I know more than I do?

- There is a special abbreviation for this purpose: "etc."

Knowledge is knowing an eggplant and bell pepper are fruits.

Wisdom is not putting them in your fruit smoothie.

I just blocked the guy on Facebook for correcting my grammar.

It fealed veary gut.

- Do you know what's the adult version of "I'm telling on you."

- What?

- "I need to speak to your manager."

The things that need to have a 'PAUSE' button:

1. FRIDAY NIGHT

2. SATURDAY NIGHT

3. SUNDAY (ALL DAY)

When I stole one idea from someone, my teacher said it was a plagiarism. When I stole five ideas from five different people, my teacher said I did great research!

The teacher:

- Students, what's happened in 1882?

- (silence)

- Franklin Delano Roosevelt was born in 1882. And what's happened in 1939?

- Franklin Delano Roosevelt celebrated his 57th birthday.

- How did you find out your super-hot neighbor doesn't watch porn?

- Well, the other day, she asked me to fix her sink. At first, I was excited until I realized her sink was really broken. Then I have been fixing the damn sink for two hours. In the end, she just said 'thank you' and gave me an apple pie.

- Maybe she doesn't watch porn, but she is a fan of "The American Pie"!

- I have a dirty mind.

- How dirty is it?

- It's so dirty if you could read it, you would be having an orgasm.

- Or I would be slapping your face!

British scientists:

"People who pour milk into the bowl before cereals are the same people who comment porn videos."

The animals in the zoo think they have trained people to feed them their favorite food.

- Mama, what do I call the outside of the tree?

- Bark.

- Whoof-whoof-whoof … Okay, mom, I'll repeat the question. What do I call the outside of the tree?

My wife believes when I say that unicorns and dragons exist. But she always wants to check whether it's true when she sees the sign: "Caution. The paint is wet."

They say nothing sticks to Teflon but wait a minute, if this is true, how does Teflon stick to the frying pan?

- Woohoo, bikini season is around the corner!

- Yes. But so is the taco truck.

Today I'll begin working as a driver. They said my starting salary is $2,500. That's great for starting, but I forgot to ask how much they pay for the driving.

If God made so many stupid people, God loves stupid people.

- I've lost my job.

- Why?

- It all started the day when my ex-mother-in-law got run over by a taxi. The next day I got fired from the taxi company.

- There is something wrong with my parents.

- What do you think is wrong with them?

- They often bust into my room.

- What if they are trying to catch you cheating on them with someone else's parents?

After searching for a pair of socks in my room for twenty minutes, I realized that Google has to learn how to search for the things offline.

The boy is asking the wise man:

- What is the one piece of advice you would give to a boy like me?

- Ok, son. Remember this: if you have plans to change the world, do it now, while you are single. Once you are married, you cannot even change the TV channel.

- My best friend is a pessimist. But I love to borrow money from him.

- Why?

- He never expects I will give it back!

- I lied to my coworkers that I have a twin sister.

- What for?

- Now when I see them in public, I can pretend that I don't know them!

- You look tired.

- I had a sleepless night. Could not sleep at all.

- What's the matter?

- I was unable to put my phone down.

- Do you exercise at home?

- Yes, I do. For example, today I had five minutes of cardio trying to pick up ice cubes from the floor in my kitchen.

Grandkids asked their grandpa:

- What were your childhood dreams? Did they come true?

- I had two childhood dreams, but only one came true. My first dream was to become an astronaut which I have not become. When my mother was brushing my hair, I was also dreaming not to have any hair at all. This dream came true, as you can see!

From chat:

<John1999> Andrew, I thought you don't bang girls, only me.

<John1999> *men

<John1999> GOD DAMN, THAT WAS A TYPO.

If you meet two alien women with six boobs each, this means together they have twelve boobs. Twelve tits are a dozen tits. Two women and a dozen tits sound odd, dozen tit?

- Do you sell rat poison?

- Yes. Do you want to take it away or you brought the rats with you?

- Andrew, why did you show a middle finger to the school principal?

- I didn't show him a middle finger. My middle finger liked him, and he gave him a standing ovation.

Every bottle with alcohol should contain the warning that alcohol consumption may make you think you are a great dancer and singer.

Two friends decided to drink coffee at some entertainment center in Manhattan. Twenty minutes later, the waiter brought them a bill for $115.

- Are you kidding? Since when two cups of coffee cost $115?

- What coffee? Ahh… coffee… Coffee is free. That's your parking ticket.

My son told me he is gay.

In a year he said it was a joke.

I asked him why did he joke like this. He replied that otherwise, I wouldn't let him inviting girls to his bedroom.

- How do I make my girlfriend angry?

- I have an idea. Find out what she wants, something like a skirt or a dress. Then buy it in XXXL size and leave it with a sweet note. She will be mad as hell!

Marriage without kids is two people sleeping together and asking each other where you want to eat or what you want to do on the weekend.

Until one of them dies!

A drunken priest asks a question at the wedding:

- Do you take Forrest Banks as your lawful husband?

- Yes, I do.

- I have a feeling you are lying, but okay.

Stevie Wonder married and divorced twice.

His ex-wives must have been doing a lot of s**t to a man who hasn't ever seen them if he never wanted to see them again.

I need white noise to fall asleep. That's why I hired my younger brother to stand by my bed while I sleep and say, "All lives matter."

All Sundays should have warning signs:

"FALLING ASLEEP ON SUNDAY CAUSES MONDAY."

- My husband never remembers my birth date. What should I do?

- Remind him a few days in advance. You may even do it several times a year. He won't notice anyway, and you'll get extra presents and birthday celebrations.

During the exam in the medical college, everyone is writing something, while one of the students is looking at the window. Professor:

- Mr. Ward, we have an exam here. Why aren't you writing anything?

- I have a problem with diarrhea.

- Oh, maybe you should go home this time. I'll let you pass the exam the next week with another group.

- Professor, I mean I'm having a problem spelling this word.

Two second-graders were playing Frisbee by a stream. One of the boys ran to the bush to get the Frisbee and saw a naked woman bathing naked on the sand behind the bush. The second boy also came, and they both started looking at the naked woman. Suddenly one of the boys took off running. The other one didn't know what happened, but he also took off. When they were far away from there, they finally stopped. And the second boy asked his friend:

- What happened? Why did you run away?

- Mother told me if I ever saw a naked woman, I would turn to stone. I thought it was a joke, but when I was looking at this woman, I felt a part of me started getting hard. I freaked out and ran.

- What do you call the thing that has six balls and can rape some poor idiots?

- Lottery.

"Don't hesitate! Send him the twentieth unanswered text message! Do it," – said your sixth cocktail tonight.

I forgot to lock my smartphone before putting it in the pocket.

Five minutes later, I took it out of my pocket to find out I have just broken up with my girlfriend, followed Justin Bieber on Twitter, and joined North Korean Communist Party.

At the funeral:

- Priest, what is the Wi-Fi password here?

- Boy, respect the dead!

- Do you spell it with a capital B?

Thai woman marries American man, but she can't speak English, and he can't speak Thai. She goes to English speaking class which is known for being highly effective for Thai people. In the evening after the first class the wife waits in the kitchen with a hot dinner. The door opens, and the husband walks in. Suddenly, his wife says without an accent:

- Hi, darling! Welcome home. Dinner is ready.

- Hi, sweetheart! I'm so glad you can speak English! It's a miracle!

- Yes. How was your day, darling?

- It was fine, but I'm very tired.

- Rest in peace!

- How to fail a job interview?

- Tell them they can get your reference from Margarita, Jose Cuervo, and Jack Daniels.

- Doctor, will my wife be able to sing in the opera after the surgery?

- Sure. It's surgical removal of the appendix. I guarantee she will be able to sing in the opera.

- Doctor, that's great! My wife is deaf-mute since her birth, but she always dreamt of singing in the opera. I wish we knew about this surgery earlier!

If people from Finland are Finns, and people from Poland are Poles, people from Holland must be Holes.

- What do you call a puppy thrown in the washing machine and never found again?

- Socks.

- I don't like your tattoos. Women with tattoos look vulgar.

- Did you just hear that? My tattoos don't like you either.

EVIAN water is one of the most expensive fresh waters in the world. People who buy a small bottle for $2 think they get the healthiest water from the mountains of France. However, I figured out why these people are buying such expensive water. You'll know the truth once you read EVIAN backward – people are NAIVE.

When I was eight, I watched "The Simpsons," and Marge Simpson celebrated her 34th birthday. Yesterday I watched "The Simpsons." I am 34 now. So is Marge.

- What are you going to do if you win $1 million in a lottery?

- First of all, I will pay for my college loans. Then I will take the remaining $30 and will take my girlfriend to Starbucks or something.

- Dad, how do I find out whether I have become a successful man or not?

- Look at your wife. If you are earning more than she currently can spend, you are a successful man.

- What's the difference between fried eggs and pea soup?

- All people can fry eggs.

On her 35th birthday, Sandra was still single without a chance to marry a prince she has been looking for the past 20 years.

That's when she twitted: "Is anybody looking for US citizenship?"

- Why do you think this mechanic has a crush on you?

- He told me to keep that rear end lubed!

- I can't afford to kiss losers.

- Why?

- My Giorgio Armani lipstick costs $38.

My wife can't live without shopping! Unfortunately, her health insurance doesn't cover retail therapy.

- Did you know that jellyfish survived for more than 500 million years, and they don't even have brains?

- Well, that's good news for 90 percent of population.

Last week I decided to follow DIET. She didn't follow me back, so I decided to unfollow her. At least I've tried!

The teacher asks his little students:

- How many of you have pets? Oh, I see many of you. Michael, what pet do you own?

- I have a Labrador Retriever whose name is Mitch.

- Awesome. Vic, what pet do you have?

- I have a parrot. Her name is Kiwi.

- That's a nice name. Marshall, what animal do you have?

- My mother has a cat. I don't know her name because I hate cats. When I grow up, I'll get something exotic.

- Like iguana?

- No, maybe a stripper.

- Angela, I saw your son was buying a book "How to Bring Up a Child." I didn't know a nine-year-old boy can be interested in books like this.

- Yes, I asked him today what he was doing with this book. He is trying to figure out whether we raise him in a proper way or not.

"I hate tacos and enchiladas!" – said no Jose Miguel ever.

- Why are you nice at work and such an a**hole at home?

- I get paid for being nice at work.

- Honey, I want you to do something sexy right now.

- For example?

- Shut up!

Why do ugly girls never tag their hot friends on photos?

- Why have you restricted access to your Instagram page?

- I wanted to make sure Santa won't see it.

- Oh yes. If he sees your Instagram pics, he'll bring you new clothes and a bible.

- Do I smell like weed?

- Nope.

- No, you are fine.

Never ask people who smell like weed, whether you smell like weed or not.

- Mom, is it alright to give up my seat to a lady on the bus?

- Yes, son.

- Today daddy asked me to give up my seat to some woman, and I was disappointed.

- Why?

- I was sitting on daddy's lap.

In the middle of the class, the cat jumped out of the backpack of one of the students. The teacher was mad. He sent the boy to the principal:

- Shame on you, Arnie. You brought the cat to school. The animal could have died in your backpack. And you should have known that you can never bring animals to the class!

- I am sorry, Mr. Lane, but I had no choice. I saved my cat's life.

- What do you mean?

- When I was getting ready to school in the morning, I've heard my dad told my mom in the bedroom, "As soon as Arnie leaves, I will eat that pussy!"

- What's the craziest thing about social media?

- When my friends post photos of their babies ten times a day, I have a feeling that I'm raising all these kids as well!

The seven-year-old girl is asking her mother:

- Mom, what is sex?

The woman decides to explain everything in details to make sure her daughter gets the information in the safest possible way. The girl listens without interruption and asks her mother again:

- Ok, Mom, I got it. Am I supposed to draw this in a tiny box of the admission form?

When I argue with my wife, in two minutes I realize it's the same thing as dealing with Microsoft license agreement. Whatever it says, in the end, you have only one option: "YES, I AGREE."

- What's wrong with your wife?

- She is in a bad mood.

- Since when?

- Since the day I married her.

- Grandpa, what is a misunderstanding?

- It's better to hear an example. When I was twenty-two, I took a vow of celibacy. However, your grandma called them "a marriage vow."

- My least favorite day of the week is SMONDAY.

- I've never heard of SMONDAY!

- It's the moment when Sunday stops feeling like a day off, and you start thinking about all crap you will have to do at work on Monday.

- Why are you leaving your wife?

- Today she gave birth to twin girls, but they are not my daughters.

- What? How do you know?

- It takes nine months for a baby to be born. So it takes 18 months for twins to be born. And we didn't even know each other 18 months ago!

A young man came to a man of wisdom.

- You are a very clever man. Tell me how I should overcome my fear. I am afraid to die alone. What should I do?

In a minute of silence, the man of wisdom replied:

- You should become a pilot or a bus driver.

If the banks are rich and they trust their clients, why do they chain their pens?

My wife said when she would walk into the house, I must finish playing Xbox, clean the house, and make soup. There was no way I could accomplish any of these three missions on time, so I called a locksmith, and he changed the locks.

Professor:

- Anyone knows why did this young man leave the classroom without my permission?

- Oh, don't worry, Professor. We live in the same room, and I know him well. He didn't mean to offend you. He is just sleepwalking.

- Are you free tomorrow?

- Tomorrow I'm very expensive.

- I saw five men kicking my mother-in-law.

- Did you help?

- No, five men are enough for her.

- Daddy, what is college like?

- College is like looking both ways before you cross the street and then getting hit by an air stone.

Funny facts about eating at home:

1. Cooking takes on average 7 hours a day.

2. Eating takes on average 10 seconds per meal.

3. Washing dishes never ends.

Fact: there are more than 2 million species of bugs on Earth.

It's even more bugs than Windows 10 has!

If duck season is the season when you can shoot ducks, are we supposed to shoot tourists during the tourist season?

About 13% of Americans are either vegan or vegetarian.

About 87% of Americans are sick of hearing about this kind of stuff.

The man has a heart attack in a supermarket. Immediately several people reach him. One guy holds his head and yells:

- Someone call 911! Is anyone here a doctor?

Vegan replies:

- I'm a vegan.

- What are you doing on this photo?

- Learning how to measure temperature in my health science class.

- Wait, you are holding the thermometer in your mouth. And that's a rectal thermometer.

At school:

- Children, how many seasons do you know?

- Four.

- Five.

- Who said five? Why do you think so?

- Ask my dad, who works for a tax company! We have spring, summer, fall, winter, and income tax season.

- What's your favorite season?

- The season of hard nipples.

- Some gas stations lock their bathrooms.

- Why?

- They are afraid someone will clean it.

- Man, you look exhausted. I was watching you from my room. You were staring at the windows for ten minutes without moving.

- Staring at the windows? Never mind, I just have too many tabs open.

The question at school:

- Who can tell me what is the fastest land animal? Okay… Ron.

- My dad is faster than any animal when mom is about to go through his phone.

There is an unspoken rule for ladies wearing animal print yoga pants, such as the leopard, panda, or elephant. You have to weigh less than the animal on your yoga pants.

High waist jeans look good on some skinny girls.

The ones with big stomachs in high waist pants often look like kangaroos.

A vegan, a crossfitter, and an atheist walk into a bar.

In ten seconds, everyone in the bar knows who they are.

Never hit a man with a ponytail. Hit him with a fist.

- I was going to take your jacket to the laundry and accidentally found this small plastic bag with a strand of hair. May I ask you why do you need a plastic bag with hair in your pocket?

- Oh, I always have it with me. In case my food is too pricey, I put some hair on the plate and take this food off my bill.

- My doctor prescribed me to play a new drinking game.

- Wow! I'd like to hear more!

- I'm supposed to drink a couple of shots of water every single hour. He said it will make me hydrated and will cure my kidney.

- It's not what I expected to hear.

Next time you go to a restaurant, order your food and then ask for tomato smoothie in the end. Enjoy the waiter's reaction. Then tell him that's how people call ketchup in another state.

What if in 50 years from now you will be listening to the music that is popular today? People will say you are listening to some old crap. And you will say they need to respect the old classical songs. And then you will choose the next track, and it's going to be something "classical" like "Bouncing on my d*ck" by Tyga.

- Why are you so mad?

- It's all because of my neighbors. What are they thinking of? I am getting sick of their crappy Wi-Fi!

I love long walks. And especially when they are taken by people who bother me.

- I have a very good habit. I always keep a bottle of wine in the fridge for special occasions. It often helps me a lot, like today.

- What's today's special occasion?

- Tuesday.

- What is your favorite drink?

- I love water. Especially frozen into cubes and surrounded by whiskey completely.

Yesterday I wanted to buy a new DVD with a horror movie at Walmart. The salesmen told me they don't sell explicit videos. I asked them how come selling explicit videos in Walmart is bad, but selling guns and ammo in Walmart is okay? They had nothing to say!

Some of the songs are too tearful! I think if The Weeknd, Drake, and Adelle make a song, I will end up missing my ex-girlfriend from the kindergarten.

- What's your favorite salad?

- A chicken seizure salad.

- Sounds dangerous!

- What do you mean when you write IDGAF?

- I don't give away food.

- How should you act the very next day after you come home very late and drunk, break your mother's favorite vase in the middle of a night and wake everyone up, so everyone can see how drunk you are?

- Stay in bed as long as possible. Everyone will start thinking you what if you are dead and they will be less pissed off.

- My name is Gina. I like social media, parties, gossips, and these kinds of things.

- What's your occupation, Gina?

- I am an unofficial private investigator.

- I've seen a very expensive trick today.

- What trick?

- A magician in a white coat put some metal into my mouth and pulled Visa Platinum card out of my pocket.

- Toby, why do you wear this strange earring? I know you are married, but it looks so gay.

- Freddy, I am not gay. I have been wearing this female earring since the day when my wife had found it in our bed.

- Do you like to watch porn?

- Yes, but I've never actually made it to the end. What happens in the end? Do they get married or something?

The girl was crying because of the broken nail. I asked:

- How can I help you?

- The only thing that can help me is a hug… e pizza and a six-pack of beer.

- How can you describe yourself in bed?

- The animal.

- A lion? A rabbit?

- A koala. I can sleep for up to 22 hours a day!

If you give my Grandma a bowl of spaghetti and chopsticks, she can make you a spaghetti scarf.

- I'm a school bus driver, and I want to quit my job. It's just too nerve-racking! I'll do something less emotional this time.

- What do you want to be?

- A bomb disarmer.

Sex on the computer cannot hurt anyone. Unless someone falls off.

- You have serious mental problems.

- Who told you this? Let me guess… Was it your imaginary friend?

- I thought I have an appointment with the doctor that cures insomnia.

- That's right. It's me.

- But you are wearing a Superman costume, and the name on your badge is "Dick."

- Yes, my name is Dick Superman, and I cure insomnia like a pro!

At court:

- Mr. Erod Chakamolt, why didn't you pay your phone bills for a year?

- Your honor, I immigrated to the United States because people were saying this country is committed to free speech. Why should I pay phone bills if I know we have freedom of speech here?

- Honey, what is "daylight savings?"

- Do you remember a few nights ago we were having sex for one hour and ten minutes?

- It was only ten minutes.

- The daylight savings adds an hour!

- Help! I'm pregnant. Parents don't know. They are going to kill me! I am sixteen. What should I do?

- Call MTV.

- I went fishing in Montana last month.

- How was it?

- Amazing! I caught a three-feet carp, but I had to let it go.

- Three-feet carp? You are such a liar! Carps don't have any feet!

- When I'm looking at my ex-girlfriend's Facebook, I have a feeling she has a permanent Valentine's Day.

- What's her Valentine's name?

- Alcohol.

When I own a convenience store, I'll sell condoms along with the other party supplies.

- Darling, can you make breakfast for me?

- Sorry, I'm sick today.

- And what if I carry you to the kitchen?

- Once upon a time, I sent a message to my girlfriend: "I want to marry you, baby!"

- YOU? It's the most unbelievable story I've ever heard! When did it happen?

- Well, I was about to be released from prison, and I needed a place to stay for a while.

- What do you call a hot lady having sex with a stand-up comedian?

- Pretty f**king funny.

- How was your trip to Amsterdam? Is it true they have drugs, alcohol, and prostitutes all around?

- I've seen it all, I've done it all, but I don't remember anything.

- Dude, you look exhausted. Take a shower. You should have told me you plan to go for a run.

- It wasn't on my to-do list. Until those cops came out of nowhere!

- Why do you always date single moms with sons?

- Here is the thing. I like to play videogames after sex. Single moms with sons always have Xbox or PlayStation at their houses.

- You also like good food, right?

- Yes…

- My grandpa is single now. He has five grandchildren and an Xbox. I hope you are not going to marry him because he is also a great chef!

- You repeat the same mistakes all the time. How can you date your ex-ex-ex-ex-girlfriend for the fifth time after you broke up with this slut four times already?

- When a mistake is repeated so often, it's called a tradition.

- Okay, we have taco Tuesday. I need some other food day of the week ideas. Do you have any?

- Taco Wednesday, taco Thursday, taco Friday...

Scientific research shows when people clean their houses, they do 3% cleaning, 7% complaining about life, and 90% playing with the stuff they have just found.

People often complain that burgers and chicken nuggets on the billboards look the way better than in reality. I agree with that.

But let's be honest. Have a look at your Instagram profile picture. And then look in the mirror.

Our wedding night was SO GOOD that all our neighbors had a cigarette.

- How do you satisfy any woman?

- You need to have 3.5-inches long thing in your pants. It doesn't matter whether it's MasterCard, Visa, Discover, or American Express.

Somehow my friends keep up with the lives of all these MTV stars, actors, football players, and the other celebrities.

Dudes, I can't even keep up with a lighter.

- Look at yourself. You are drunk!

- Yep.

- Where have you been drinking?

- At home.

- You've been drinking alone?

- I cannot be drinking alone if my parrot is home.

"SO BORED" and "SOBER" sound similar.

I bet there must be a reason for this!

A woman sits at the bar all alone. The drunken man asks her:

- Oh, my God! You must be single, right?

- If the lady has a drink at the bar, you assume she is single?

- No, I did not mean this. You are just very ugly!

- What do you call a blonde who has got two brain cells?

- Pregnant.

- Excuse me. There is no price tag on this baby jacuzzi. How much it costs?

- Sir, it is a crockpot.

- If a snail doesn't have a shell, is it naked or homeless?

- It's dead.

Doctor:

- Your health issues can be related to the quality of your sleep. Do you sleep well?

- As far as I can remember, I close my eyes when I sneeze.

My therapist:

- I think it's the right time to start working on your SELF LOVE!

- Doc, I can't do it in front of you.

Professor:

- It's embarrassing. You are chewing gum!

- No, Sir. I'm your student, Eddie Tucker.

- What should I do if my son hates meat?

- Relax. He might be a veterinarian.

My best friend borrowed $50 from me. A few days later, my wife ran off with my best friend.

I'm still missing my $50.

Many girls at my college say they hate fake handbags and shoes.

But look at them. The same girls love their fake hair, fake lips, fake tits, and fake butts.

During the funeral, the dead guy stands up in the coffin. Everyone freezes. The guy says:

- I apologize for interrupting you. I have just realized I forgot my earphones. Can I borrow someone's?

- Oh, I'm so tired!

- You are too young to be tired, girl.

- You are too old to be alive, but here we are!

- Why did you go to the movie theater without your boyfriend?

- He is now in a relationship with something else.

- Something else? You mean "someone else?" What's her name?

- Marijuana.

I've met a pretty woman on my way from New York to Moscow. I almost fell in love with her. But suddenly, she started clapping when the plane landed.

My Mom only lets my boyfriend into my bedroom when we do the math.

But when we do math with him, we always get 69.

A young man asks a female librarian:

- Good morning, do you have a new book on small penises?

- Sorry, it's not in yet.

- Yes, that's the name of the book that I need!

- How can I pick up a hot and drunk girl?

- Park your car outside a fancy bar late in the evening. Wait until some hot chick approaches your car and asks whether you are her uber driver.

- I finally have a housekeeper.

- Congrats. Is she hot?

- You know her. It's my ex-wife.

- What? How is it possible that your ex-wife is your housekeeper?

- It's because she now keeps my house.

A man walks into the bedroom. His new girlfriend is waiting naked for him in bed. The man is holding a parrot.

- Mike, why are you holding a parrot? Let it go and come to me.

- It is the elephant I want to have sex with. What do you think?

- It's not the elephant. It's a parrot.

- Can you please shut up? I'm talking to my parrot.

Surprise sex is a perfect thing to wake up to.

P.S. Unless you are in prison.

REVIEWS

Your reviews are extremely important!

If you enjoyed reading this book, please consider leaving me **a short review**. That really is the best way you can help new readers find my book. I would appreciate it!

Made in the USA
Monee, IL
09 May 2020